TEAM PLANET!

PROTECT OCEANS

BY LOUISE SPILSBURY AND VICTOR MEDINA

FRANKLIN WATTS
LONDON · SYDNEY

unesco

Published by the United Nations Educational, Scientific and Cultural Organization (UNESCO), 7, place de Fontenoy, 75352 Paris 07 SP, France, and Hodder & Stoughton Limited (on behalf of its publishing imprint Franklin Watts, a division of Hachette Children's Group), Carmelite House, 50 Victoria Embankment, London EC4Y 0DZ, United Kingdom.

© UNESCO and Hodder & Stoughton Limited (on behalf of its publishing imprint Franklin Watts, a division of Hachette Children's Group), 2025

Hodder and Stoughton ISBNs: 978 1 4451 8990 1 (hardback) 978 1 4451 8991 8 (paperback)

One year following first publication of this book, electronic files of the content will be available under the terms of a CC-BY-NC-ND 3.0 IGO license whereby use and re-distribution of the Work are allowed on the basis that there is a superimposed watermark across each page to say 'Not for commercial use', the original source is properly quoted and each recipient may use the Work only under the terms of the CC-BYNC-ND 3.0 IGO license. Commercial re-distribution and derivative works are not allowed under this license without prior authorization from UNESCO and Hodder & Stoughton Limited. By using the content of this publication, the users accept to be bound by the terms of use of the UNESCO Open Access Repository (www.unesco.org/open-access/terms-use-ccbyncnd-en).

The designations employed and the presentation of material throughout this publication do not imply the expression of any opinion whatsoever on the part of UNESCO concerning the legal status of any country, territory, city or area or of its authorities, or concerning the delimitation of its frontiers or boundaries.

The ideas and opinions expressed in this publication are those of the author; they are not necessarily those of UNESCO and do not commit the Organization.

Editor: Victoria Brooker
Designer: Peter Scoulding
Illustrations: Victor Medina
Picture research: Diana Morris

Printed and bound in China

Franklin Watts
An imprint of
Hachette Children's Group
Part of Hodder and Stoughton
Carmelite House
50 Victoria Embankment
London EC4Y 0DZ

An Hachette UK company.
www.hachette.co.uk
www.hachettechildrens.co.uk

The authorised representative in the EEA is Hachette Ireland, 8 Castlecourt Centre, Dublin 15, D15 XTP3, Ireland (email: info@hbgi.ie)

Picture credits:
Alamy: Robert Gilhooly 26b; ImageBroker.com GMBh &- Co.KG 17b; Inga Spence 7.
iStock: Makasana 20-21t.
Nature PL: Richard Herrmann 14-15; Alex Mustard 12; Will Watson 25b; Norbert Wu 22.
Shutterstock: Mohamed Abdulraheem 8; Alexander-stock23 5t; bekirevren10;
Michael Bogner 25t; Damsea 13; Davdeka 6; Moshe Einhorn 29; Leonardo Gonzalez 24-25b; Yeongsik Im 9t; Beat J Korner f cover r, 3b, 16-17; Gennadily Naumov 27t; Smarta 30;
TasfotoNL 21b; Timsimages f cover l, 23; Eriq Walker 18-19; wild_and_free_naturephoto 9b.
The Argo Program: https://argo.ucsd.edu PD 11.
UNDP: 28
Wikimedia: Museum de Geneve CCA-SA 3.0 24c.

Every effort has been made to clear copyright. Should there be any inadvertent omission, please apply to the publisher for rectification.

INFORMATION SOURCES AND DISCLAIMER
Statistical information in this book has been taken, as far as possible, from the websites and publications of UNESCO and other United Nations agencies. The information given is as up-to-date as possible at the time of printing this book. However, the on-going management of UNESCO sites and historic events means that some of the facts and figures are liable to change.

CONTENTS

ALL ABOUT THE OCEAN	4
OCEAN POLLUTION	6
ALDABRA ATOLL, SEYCHELLES	8
THE WARMING OCEAN	10
SHARK BAY, WESTERN AUSTRALIA	12
FOODS FROM THE OCEAN	14
BELIZE BARRIER REEF RESERVE SYSTEM, BELIZE	16
THE OCEAN AND INDUSTRY	18
WADDEN SEA, DENMARK, GERMANY, KINGDOM OF THE NETHERLANDS	20
EXPLORING THE OCEAN	22
ARCHIPIÉLAGO DE REVILLAGIGEDO, MEXICO	24
TSUNAMIS AND OCEAN HAZARDS	26
TANJUNG BENOA, INDONESIA	28
THE FUTURE OF THE OCEAN	30
UNESCO IN ACTION	31
RESOURCES AND INDEX	32

All About the Ocean

Astronauts who look down on our planet from space say it looks like a big blue ball! That's because more than two-thirds of Earth is covered by the ocean. This vast area of salty seawater gives all of us life, no matter where we live. Team Planet is travelling around the world to find out how the ocean helps us and how and why we need to help the ocean. Come along for the ride!

Hop on board!

From the shallow waters we paddle in at the coast, to the open ocean where ships ride rough waves, and to the dark, hidden world of the deep ocean, the ocean is home to a wonderful variety of wildlife. The different parts of the ocean also provide people with many of the resources we need, from food and medicine, to oil we use for electricity and fuel and materials we use to make things such as TVs and smartphones. It also provides millions of people with work!

We transport goods and people over the ocean in ships and we have great fun in and on the ocean, too.

Copenhagen, Denmark

The ocean drives the world's weather and climate. Without it we would not have the rain that gives plants and animals, including us, life and provides the freshwater that pours from our taps. The ocean even provides most of the oxygen we breathe. However, the ocean ecosystem is under threat as people alter, damage or pollute it, putting its health and future at risk.

UNESCO is a global organization that is helping to protect the ocean. UNESCO stands for the United Nations Educational, Scientific and Cultural Organization. The countries in UNESCO work together to keep the ocean healthy for people, wildlife and the planet.

OCEAN POLLUTION

One of the biggest threats to the ocean is pollution. People dump all sorts of waste into the waters that cover our planet. Sometimes this is accidentally, but sometimes it is on purpose. This waste causes serious problems for the ocean, the wildlife living in it and us.

Humans are responsible for a variety of ocean pollution. Dirt and chemicals wash down drainpipes from homes, streets or factories. Sewage from water treatment systems and chemicals from farm fields can wash into oceans. Oil from ships, planes and other vehicles leaks into our waters, too. Plastic waste, such as fishing nets, plastic bags, bottles, straws and containers, stays in the ocean for hundreds of years because, unlike some other forms of waste, plastic does not rot away or biodegrade within a human lifetime.

Even if we live far from the coast, the waste we produce flows from the land into drains and sewers, into streams and then rivers that flow into the ocean.

HOT SPOT!

Ocean pollution is a disaster for ocean wildlife. Plastic waste alone kills many thousands of fish, whales, turtles, seabirds and other ocean animals each year. Not to mention the microplastic that is already making its way into human food. Ocean animals die because they mistake the plastics for food or get entangled in it. Oil spills clog fur and feathers, stopping birds and animals from keeping warm.

These sealions were in danger because they had plastic waste trapped around their necks. Rescuers removed the plastic and nursed them back to health. Now they're returning the animals to the ocean where they belong.

California, USA

ALDABRA ATOLL, SEYCHELLES

When members of Team Planet arrived at the remote World Heritage site at Aldabra Atoll in the Seychelles, they were surprised to find very few people on these coral islands but lots of plastic litter! Where did it all come from?

Tonnes of plastic pollution are washed onto these shores by ocean currents. It's a big threat to the wildlife here. Beaches clogged with plastic make it hard for turtles to bury their eggs under the sand and when baby turtles hatch out they struggle to get to the ocean to feed because of the waste.

Some of the marine turtles that live here get tangled in or swallow plastic waste.

"Workers removed 25 tons of waste from the beaches, including 60,000 plastic flip-flops! Sadly, there is still a lot of plastic there."

The United Nations (UN) is tackling ocean plastic pollution through action, education and research. On this atoll, 12 volunteers from the Seychelles and England spent five weeks collecting waste from the beaches, which was collected and removed by ship. Pictures and stories about the plastic waste and its threat to wildlife appeared on news outlets around the world and were shown at important meetings of world leaders.

This taught people to think about the environment and stop using throwaway plastic items. Scientists studied the plastic collected from the beaches and discovered that most of it came from places far from the islands. Finding out where the plastic comes from and how much there is helps the countries responsible to know what waste to reduce.

"A lot of the waste was fishing gear. This showed big fishing boat companies that to protect the fish they catch they need to reduce the waste they make, too."

THE WARMING OCEAN

Life on Earth exists because oceans help to keep our planet warm enough for living things to survive. Seawater absorbs heat from Earth's atmosphere and ocean currents move it around the planet, stopping different places from getting too cold or too hot. The problem is that as climate change warms the atmosphere, the ocean absorbs more heat. A warming ocean is a threat to ocean food chains and us.

Krill may be small animals but they are hugely important. The giant blue whale feeds mainly on krill. Many of the fish we eat, such as sardine and salmon, eat krill, too.

Some ocean animals cannot survive in a warmer ocean. Tiny shrimp-like krill live in freezing cold water. They stop having young when water gets warmer. This reduces the food for fish, seals, whales and many other ocean animals that eat krill, or eat the smaller animals that feed on krill. It also affects people who eat fish and other seafood that need krill to survive.

ARGO is a network of around 4,000 floats that drift around the ocean measuring water temperature and acidity. Scientists all over the world use the information they collect to study the warming ocean.

HOT SPOT!

As well as absorbing heat, the ocean also soaks up carbon dioxide, a gas that causes climate change. This changes the water's chemical balance, making it more acidic. Young shellfish cannot form the strong shells they need to survive in acidic water. Shellfish are at the start of many ocean food chains. Losing them disrupts the food supply for other ocean animals – and us.

Dugongs can stay underwater for up to six minutes at a time and eat up to 30 kg of seagrass a day. That's about the same as 60 lettuces!

Shark Bay, Western Australia

The World Heritage site Shark Bay, Western Australia is so-called because of the numerous sharks here, but Team Planet are investigating different animals: dugongs. One of the world's largest populations of dugong live among the incredible underwater seagrass meadows here.

Dugongs are nicknamed sea cows because they graze on seagrass day and night. It's all they eat! Seagrasses are not only important to dugongs. These plants also provide shelter for young fish to live safely while they grow, until they are able to swim fast to escape predators that try to eat them. The problem is that climate change is causing ocean heatwaves here. When the water temperature gets too high, seagrasses cannot survive. If seagrasses die, the dugongs, crabs, turtles and other animals that feed on them may die as well.

Seagrasses are important for people and the planet, too. They help to reduce the impact of climate change by absorbing large amounts of carbon from the atmosphere and the ocean. UNESCO has calculated how much carbon the seagrass meadows at Shark Bay, Western Australia World Heritage site store. By showing how important they are, UNESCO encourages countries to invest in their conservation and restoration.

The seagrass meadow at Shark Bay is formed from just one plant that has spread over 180 km. It is believed to be the largest known plant on Earth!

FOODS FROM THE OCEAN

The most important foods we get from the ocean are fish and shellfish. Billions of people around the world rely on fish for protein, which is needed to build, maintain and replace the tissues that make up the different parts of our bodies.

Bluefin tuna are big fish that dive deep and swim quickly in oceans all over the world. Some countries have put limits on the amount of bluefin tuna that can be caught in an attempt to stop these fish disappearing from our planet forever due to overfishing.

Ocean fish are important in other ways, too. Millions of people around the world earn a living by catching, transporting fish or preparing fish to eat. And up to one third of all the fish harvested from the ocean is turned into food for farm animals that humans eat.

Catching fish isn't necessarily bad for the ocean, except when big fishing boats catch too many of one type or species of fish at one time. This is called overfishing. Overfishing means there are not enough adult fish left in the ocean to have young. That puts some fish species at risk of extinction – dying out altogether.

HOT SPOT!

Another problem with the huge fishing nets and long lines that cause overfishing is bycatch. Bycatch includes animals such as dolphins, turtles and seabirds that get hooked up or entangled in fishing lines or nets and get hauled in with the fish people want to catch. The bycatch animals that fishing companies cannot sell are usually thrown overboard, dead or dying.

Belize Barrier Reef Reserve System, Belize

Team Planet are in Belize to dive into the mystery of how saving one colourful fish can help to keep an entire coral reef healthy!

The beautiful Belize Barrier Reef Reserve System, Belize, is a UNESCO World Heritage site. This stunning coral reef system is the second largest in the world. It is made up of vibrant and brightly coloured corals and is home to fluorescent fish and many other animals, including turtles, manatees and American crocodiles. It is also important to local people who earn a living from fishing and tourism here.

UNESCO is helping to protect the stunning coral reefs that make up the Belize Barrier Reef Reserve System to help the animals and the local people who rely on it.

Many coral reefs like this one are under threat. The warmer waters caused by climate change destroy corals, which turn white and die. To save the Belize reef system from bleaching like this, tour guides, fishers, divers and other volunteers are trained to plant new coral here to keep it alive.

Scientists then discovered overfishing of parrotfish was causing a problem too. Parrotfish are beautifully coloured fish that spend most of their time scraping algae from coral reefs. They keep corals clean. Because they were overfished, there was too much algae and it started to smother the coral reefs. Parrotfish are now protected, so there are more parrotfish to eat more algae and keep the corals clean.

Parrotfish are named for their strong mouth and jaws that look like a parrot's beak!

THE OCEAN AND INDUSTRY

We think of the ocean as a wild and natural place, but the truth is more and more of it is being taken over by industries. As the world's population grows and more industries move into the ocean, this is becoming a serious problem.

Ships lay cables on the ocean floor to carry data around the world. Oil and gas companies drill for fossil fuels and mining companies dig up sand and gravel for building and metals such as copper, which is used to make mobile phones. Ships carrying people, oil and other cargo crisscross the ocean, too.

> Ocean reserves are areas of the ocean protected by law. Fishing and mining are banned and the number of people who can visit is limited so ocean animals can live safely and undisturbed.

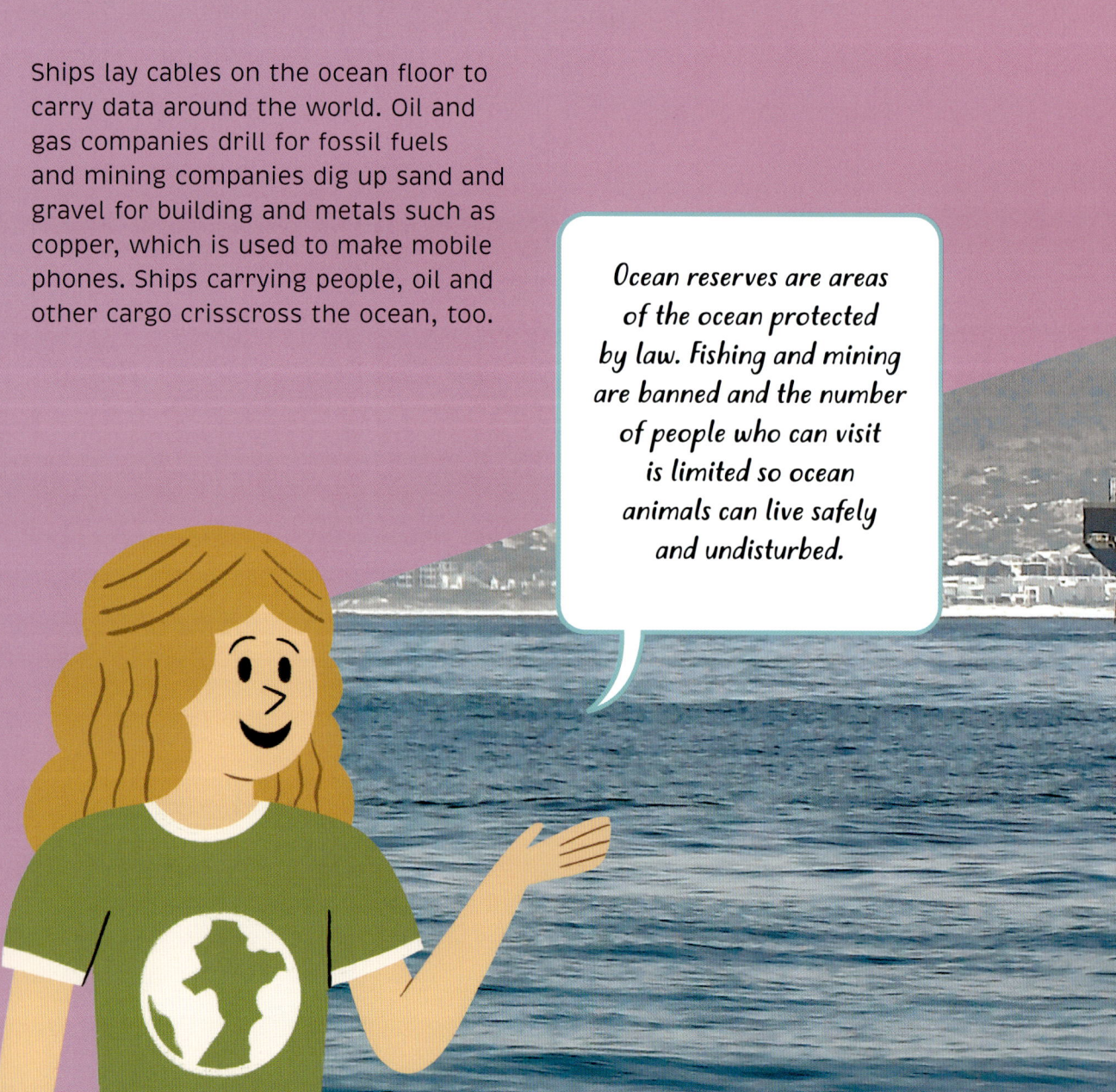

As more industries use the ocean they spread into the high seas, far from the waters 320 km beyond their shorelines that belong to individual countries. The high seas cover two-thirds of the ocean and belong to us all. The UN is working to persuade countries around the planet to agree to rules to protect the high seas and create protected areas of the open ocean where industries are banned.

HOT SPOT!

Ocean industries cause a variety of problems. They release greenhouse gases that contribute to climate change and destroy wildlife habitats. Noise from shipping and drilling travels long distances in water and stops ocean animals hearing sounds such as those that help them avoid predators. Waste from industries such as oil spills can kill ocean animals.

WADDEN SEA,
DENMARK, GERMANY, KINGDOM OF THE NETHERLANDS

The Wadden Sea World Heritage Site is the largest tidal flat system in the world. It is an enormous area of muddy shores and sandy islands that are covered and uncovered by the rise and fall of ocean tides twice a day. It is so big it extends along the coasts of three countries: Denmark, Germany and Kingdom of the Netherlands.

Millions of birds stop here on their long migratory flights around the globe and many seals live here or come to feed, rest and have young. Young fish grow up here and animals such as worms, shrimps and crabs burrow in the mud. A tiny creature that looks like a stone is actually the spire snail, the fastest snail in the world!

"Grey seals give birth during the middle of the winter. The pups have long fur to keep them warm when cold winds whip across the mud."

UNESCO helped Denmark, Germany and the Kingdom of the Netherlands work together to agree on a plan to give tourists the best experience while also protecting the site. Each country offers guided walks and visitor centres that teach people the importance of the mudflats and how to behave while they are there. They stop tourist hotels or centres being built too close to the shore. They close areas off to visitors when necessary to protect wildlife, such as when seals are having their pups.

"Tourism is one of the most important industries in the Wadden Sea region. Tourism brings work to local people and money to help maintain the site, but could put the habitat and the wildlife at risk."

EXPLORING THE OCEAN

Parts of the deep and open ocean are still a mystery to us. Unlocking the secrets in these waters teaches us about the wildlife there and how the ocean keeps our planet healthy. It can even tell us more about human history.

Scientists think that we have identified less than a tenth of all the species in the ocean. Finding new species helps us in many ways. For example, scientists make copies of chemicals found in living things such as ocean corals to make life-saving medicines.

New underwater technologies help us to explore and find new ocean animals, like this 20-armed, multiple-legged feather star from the Antarctic.

It is important to find and protect shipwrecks because they provide valuable information about the past.

Technology such as underwater robots helps to locate shipwrecks. Shipwrecks are like time capsules that provide a complete snapshot of life at the time of sinking. Some of the 3 million wrecks that lie on the ocean's floor are thousands of years old. Finding wrecks means people can study them and protect them from looters.

HOT SPOT!

Studying life in the ocean is essential. Phytoplankton are the base of many food chains. They produce about 70 per cent of Earth's oxygen and capture carbon from the atmosphere. Learning more about phytoplankton and how to keep these ocean plants safe keeps the planet safe too.

ARCHIPIÉLAGO DE REVILLAGIGEDO, MEXICO

This UNESCO World Heritage site consists of beautiful remote islands and their surrounding waters. The ocean here is home to some incredible wildlife, including manta rays, whales, dolphins and sharks.

These islands are the peaks of volcanoes emerging above the ocean. They are so undisturbed that some endangered species, such as the Sorocco mockingbird, are found only here and nowhere else in the world.

Team Planet is here to find out about a new scientific method being used to explore the wildlife here and how it is changing. When a fish or other animal moves through water, it leaves traces such as skin cells behind. The DNA in these traces is known as environmental DNA (eDNA). Just one litre of water may contain eDNA from hundreds of species. It tells scientists which animals visit or live here without the need to see them.

Giant manta rays live in the warm waters around the islands, feeding on plankton and small fish. Divers visit to swim with these amazing animals.

Knowing where ocean animals feed, rest and breed tells us which areas of the ocean need protection. UNESCO World Heritage sites protect marine wildlife, but as climate change heats the ocean this may cause underwater species to move away to find cooler water. Sometimes this could mean that they move beyond protected areas. Using eDNA, scientists can track where species are moving to help determine whether protected areas' boundaries need to be extended.

Studying ocean animals using eDNA is easy and cheap. Combined with research into ocean temperatures, eDNA samples can show how climate change is impacting ocean species.

TSUNAMIS AND OCEAN HAZARDS

Tsunamis and other ocean hazards can be devastating for the world's coasts, the people living there and ocean wildlife.

Tsunamis are huge, destructive waves that happen after an earthquake or volcanic eruption on the ocean floor or after huge chunks of rock or ice break off land and crash into water. These events cause enormous quantities of water to move suddenly. As the moving mass of water nears land where the ocean is shallow, it piles up. Some tsunami waves reach the height of a 12-storey building.

Large, powerful tsunamis can cause death and destruction when they hit land. UNESCO helps to set up systems to protect communities at risk of tsunamis in the world, such as warning systems and escape plans.

Harmful algal blooms are very different to tsunamis and develop much more slowly, but they are a serious ocean hazard too! Algal blooms happen when many small algae grow together into a thick soup or as a mat on the water surface. The algae can sometimes produce toxins that kill fish and other animals. These toxins can move up the food chain as the algae and smaller animals are eaten by larger animals. Eating seafood containing algal toxins can make people seriously ill too.

Most algae are harmless and an important part of the ocean, but some produce deadly toxins.

UNESCO supports research on harmful algal blooms to understand their causes, where and when they might happen and how to deal with them.

Minami Sanriku Town, Miyagi Prefecture, Japan

HOT SPOT!

As the ocean gets warmer, sea ice in the Arctic and around Greenland begins to melt. As ice melts, sea levels rise and coasts and islands are submerged. This is another major threat to coastal communities, from island countries in the Pacific to cities like New York and Venice.

27

TANJUNG BENOA, INDONESIA

The village of Tanjung Benoa on the island of Bali, Indonesia, sits beside white sandy beaches and the crystal-clear waters of the Indian Ocean. Tourists flock to enjoy the idyllic coast here, alongside locals. The problem is that this village lies in an area prone to dangerous tsunamis, with waves reaching 20 m high.

> Schoolchildren have evacuation drills to keep them safe. These children practise heading for the upper levels of a multi-storey hotel close to their classroom if they hear a tsunami warning siren.

Team Planet is here to find out how UNESCO is working with Tanjung Benoa to keep people safe. First, the coastline is studied and maps are made to show where and how far a tsunami would flood the land. This is the Tsunami Hazard Zone. Maps of evacuation routes show people the best routes to take to escape a tsunami and where to gather in safe places. Signs along evacuation routes ensure everyone knows where to go, including tourists who may be new to the area.

People are also taught about tsunami safety. They learn to leave beaches any time there is an earthquake. They practise tsunami evacuations with family, friends and neighbours. People are also encouraged to prepare an emergency kit containing water, food, a torch, a battery-powered radio and a first-aid kit and medicines they need. This should be ready to grab any time when it is necessary.

Sirens are put in place to give loud warnings to everyone when a tsunami is coming.

THE FUTURE OF THE OCEAN

People all over the world are working hard to keep the ocean safe from the threats facing it. They are creating marine reserves to protect areas of the ocean and its wildlife. They are studying ocean wildlife to see what it needs to survive and studying ocean warming to learn how to protect the ocean world from climate change.

We can all help to take care of our precious ocean. We can reduce the amount of plastic waste we make and recycle more. We can take care not to pour hazardous waste down our drains. We can also take the time to learn more about the ocean and tell other people how they can help it, too.

Tourists watching dolphins in Bali, Indonesia

It's our planet and we're all a team. The ocean is one of our planet's most precious places and we can all help to protect it!

UNESCO IN ACTION

UNESCO and the United Nations are doing all they can to safeguard the ocean for the future. Their main project is called the 'United Nations Decade of Ocean Science for Sustainable Development 2021-2030', or 'Ocean Decade' for short.

The plan is to make changes that give us and our planet the ocean we want and need by 2030. This will be a healthier ocean, which can cope with climate change. It will be an ocean in which coastal communities are safer from tsunamis and other marine hazards. They also want to ensure that everyone, from ordinary people living far from the coast to governments that make decisions that affect the ocean, understands what the ocean needs and feels connected to it.

This won't be easy. It will involve some serious challenges, from beating marine pollution to rethinking the way we use the ocean. It will need everyone on the planet to join in and do what they can to make the Ocean Decade happen.

RESOURCES

Find out about the UN's Sustainable Development Goals for the ocean:
www.un.org/sustainabledevelopment/oceans/
- Read about the Tide Turners Plastic Challenge to see if you can help too:
www.unep.org/explore-topics/education-environment/what-we-do/tide-turners-plastic-challenge
- Learn more about plastic pollution and what you can do to reduce plastic waste:
www.unep.org/interactives/beat-plastic-pollution/www.cleanseas.org/
- Learn about your rights to have a healthy ocean:
https://oneoceanhub.org/childrens-right-to-a-healthy-ocean/
- Find out what people around the world are doing on World Oceans' Day
https://unworldoceansday.org/category/youth/
Find out more about UNESCO's work here:
www.ioc.unesco.org/en
www.unesco.org/en/decades/ocean-decade
https://oceanliteracy.unesco.org/?post-types=all&sort=popular
https://whc.unesco.org/en/marine-programme/

INDEX

chains, food 10-11, 23, 27
climate 5, 10
climate change 10-13, 17, 19, 25, 30-31

dugongs 12-13

e-DNA 25

fish 7, 9-12, 14-17, 20, 25, 27
fishing 6, 9, 14-18

gases, greenhouse 11, 19

industries 18-19, 21 *see also* fishing

krill 10-11

microplastics 7

overfishing 14-15, 17
oxygen 5, 23

pollution 5-9, 30-31

reefs, coral 16-17, 22

seagrasses 12-13
shipwrecks 23

tourism 16, 21, 28, 30
tsunamis 26-29, 31

waste, plastic 6-9, 30
weather 5
wildlife 4-17, 19-27, 30